THE WISDOM YEARS

the
Wisdom
Years

Prayers & practice for finding joy
in life's second half

LORENE DUQUIN

**TWENTY-THIRD
PUBLICATIONS**
twentythirdpublications.com

Twenty-Third Publications
One Montauk Avenue, Suite 200
New London, CT 06320
(860) 437-3012 or (800) 321-0411
www.twentythirdpublications.com

Cover photo: Tasha Zalevska/Shutterstock.com
ISBN: 978-1-62785-665-2

Printed in the U.S.A.

A division of Bayard, Inc.

CONTENTS

INTRODUCTION

Amazing things happen in the second half of life. We embark on a journey toward wisdom using all of the lessons we learned from the past, all of the joys and challenges of the present, and all of our hopes and dreams for the future.

During the second half of life, we experience a new kind of freedom. Insecurities diminish. We know who we are and our strengths and weaknesses. We envision new things that we want to experience. We recognize the need to make the most out of each passing day.

But the second half of life is not without difficulties. We may encounter physical limitations. We may lose friends and loved ones. We may face situations that demand courage, understanding, insight, and the need to let go of the things that are out of our control.

At the same time, we recognize that difficulties are nothing new for us. We have faced and overcome difficulties in the first half of our lives. We learned lessons, developed survival skills, and deepened our faith. With all of our rich experiences, the second half of life unfolds before us as a new adventure.

This little book of meditations offers ideas, prayers, and practical things you can do as you journey through the second half of life. Let us begin this journey filled with the belief that we will experience God in new ways, and we will start to see the world and other people from a new perspective.

May the Holy Spirit inspire us, lead us, and protect us on this profound journey to finding new meaning, greater joy, and deeper fulfillment.

The Story
of Our Lives

Each person's life tells a unique story, starting at birth and unfolding throughout the years. Our story contains loving relationships, personal growth, successes, failures, adventures, and a lot of ordinary day-to-day moments that become more precious with the passing of time. Our faith assures us that the Lord remains with us as each chapter unfolds to guide us, encourage us, comfort us, and love us unconditionally.

PRAY

Lord, help me to understand and appreciate the story of my life. Allow me to see that throughout my life, through all the good times and all the bad times, you have remained with me and loved me with an everlasting love. Amen.

PRACTICE

Reflect on what it means to be loved unconditionally. Make a list of the times in your life when you felt God's comforting, healing, and merciful love.

Looking Back

PONDER

Looking back allows us to recognize profound lessons in life. We see the times we fell down and how we stood up again. We see people we helped and people who helped us. We see moments of great hope, times of powerful healing, and situations where the only explanation for what happened was a miracle of God's grace. It is important to remember that we can look back, but we cannot *go* back. We can cherish memories, but if we keep wishing we were back in the past, our lives stall, and we cannot move forward.

PRAY

Lord, allow me to recognize the deepest lessons in my life. Help me to see that everything in my past—the good and the bad—is a piece of a puzzle that makes me the person that I am today. Amen.

PRACTICE

Think back on the most important lessons you have learned on your journey through life. Share your life lessons with friends or family members. Ask them to share their life lessons with you.

The Second
Half of Life

PONDER

Some people dread growing older. Others insist that with age comes wisdom, a deep appreciation of life, and a new kind of freedom. When we embrace the second half of life, we can scoff at stereotypes depicting older people as forgetful, feeble, and bad-tempered. We can cling to the adage that aging is simply mind over matter: if we don't mind, it doesn't matter!

PRAY

Lord, help me to embrace aging and to grow older gracefully. Give me a deep appreciation for every moment of every day. Give me the courage to live my life to the fullest. Instill in me the gift of wisdom. Amen.

PRACTICE

Decide to do something that you have always wanted to do. It might be something easy to accomplish. Or it might be something challenging. Explore with family members or friends the ways you might proceed.

Who Am I?

PONDER

In the second half of life, we begin to understand that we are part of something bigger than ourselves. We glimpse the great mystery of life. We discover at a deep level what it means to be children of a merciful and loving God. We recognize that who *we are* in relation to God is more important than anything that *we do*. We begin to see that God's love can flow through us and touch other people.

PRAY

Lord, help me to see myself as you see me. Fill me with your love. Let me be a conduit of your love to other people—especially those who are suffering in any way or struggling with doubts and sadness. Amen.

PRACTICE

Put a stick-it note on your mirror with the words, "God's image," as a reminder that you were made in the image and likeness of God who loves you completely and unconditionally. Thank God every day for the gift of your life. Thank God for the gift of family members and friends who love you.

The Purpose of Life

Everyone is born with God-given gifts and talents. The way we use our gifts and talents gives meaning and purpose to our lives. We can use our gifts and talents to make the world a better place by helping other people and growing closer to God. We can use our gifts and talents in selfish ways by making the world a crueler place and cutting ourselves off from God. Or we can take our gifts and talents for granted and drift

12

along without any awareness of the spiritual meaning or purpose in our lives.

Lord, help me to recognize the gifts you have given to me. Guide me so that I can use my gifts and talents in ways that are pleasing to you. Reveal to me the true purpose of my life. Amen.

Ask a friend or family member to help you identify your God-given gifts and talents. Think of all the ways you used your God-given gifts throughout the first half of your life. Look for new ways that you can use your gifts for the greater glory of God in the second half of life.

What Does God Want?

God wants us to be the best person that we can be with all of our strengths and all of our weaknesses. Each one of us is unique. God does not want us to try to be someone else. God does not expect us to do things that are beyond our abilities. God leads us in ways that are life-giving for the betterment of ourselves and other people.

Lord, help me to understand where you are leading me in the second half of my life. Allow me to recognize what is life-giving for me and for the people around me. Give me the courage to be the person you want me to be. Amen.

PRACTICE

Think about the ways the Holy Spirit has prompted you throughout your life to try something new. How is the Holy Spirit nudging you now? Does this feel energizing and life-giving? If not, you may need to spend some additional time to discern what God is asking of you.

What Is Discernment?

PONDER

The process of determining what God is asking is called discernment. The word discernment means to sift apart. When we enter into discernment, we set aside time to pray and to talk with a friend, a family member, or a spiritual advisor who can help us gain insights as to where we are being led. Sometimes discernment helps us discover that God is not asking us to *do* something, but rather, God is asking us to *be* something—more loving, more compassionate, more trusting.

Lord, I feel as if you are moving me in a new direction in the second half of my life. Help me to discern what you are asking of me. Give me the courage to follow in whatever direction you lead. Amen.

PRACTICE
Start a spiritual journal. Record thoughts, inspirations, and ideas that come to you in prayer, in dreams, in conversations, or in the course of your daily activities. Share your journal with a family member, friend, or spiritual advisor who can help to recognize the movement of the Holy Spirit in your life.

Your Outlook
on Life

Our attitudes impact how we behave. People with positive attitudes tend to look on the bright side of life and anticipate that bad things are fleeting. They tend to be affirming, forward-thinking, and happy. People with negative attitudes tend to focus on things that are going badly and anticipate that bad things will continue to happen. They tend to be skeptical, cynical, and sometimes grumpy.

PRAY

Lord, help me to become a more positive person. Give me the courage to banish negative thoughts and feelings that lead to self-defeating behaviors. Allow me to believe with all my being that you can make something good come out of even the worst situations if I simply trust in you. Amen.

PRACTICE

Take an honest look at your attitudes. If you find yourself wallowing in negative thoughts, break the cycle by asking yourself how you would feel if you thought the opposite. Remind yourself that negative situations are not permanent. Trust that God will give you everything you need to overcome difficulties.

Counting Our Blessings

PONDER

When we count our blessings, we recognize the many ways that God has touched our lives. We see goodness in ourselves and in other people. We understand how the Lord walked with us in good times and in bad times. Counting our blessings helps us to develop an attitude of gratitude that leads to a deep sense of joy.

PRAY

Lord, make me aware of the many blessings you have bestowed upon me. Instill in me an attitude of gratitude. Help me to recognize your presence in the everyday moments of my life and to respond with thankfulness. Amen.

PRACTICE

Make it a point to smile every time you recognize God's presence in something that happens or in someone you encounter during the day. Every night before going to sleep, thank God for the blessings bestowed on you during the day. Keep an ongoing list of the many blessings in your life.

Staying Healthy

A well-balanced diet, regular exercise, and reduced stress will not keep us from growing older. But healthy habits can improve our quality of life by strengthening bones and muscles, increasing energy levels, improving balance, and lessening our chance of heart disease, high blood pressure, and certain types of cancer. Everyone can choose whether or not to adopt healthy habits. It is never too late to start.

PRAY

Lord, allow me to see my body as a temple of the Holy Spirit. Help me to break bad habits. Give me the strength to do whatever I need to do in order to maintain good health and well-being. Amen.

PRACTICE

Take a serious look at your lifestyle. What healthy habits do you want to continue or increase? What unhealthy habits do you need to break? Start today to make the necessary changes. Invite family members or friends to join you on the road to better health.

Managing
Stress

PONDER

Stress is our body's natural response to danger. Problems arise when we are not in danger, but tensions, worries, and fears cause the continual release of stress hormones that can harm us physically and mentally. The first step in managing stress is to recognize that stress has become a problem in our lives. Our next step is to find ways to reduce stress by practicing stress management techniques such as journaling, meditation, and physical exercise each day.

PRAY

Lord, open my eyes to the things that are causing harmful stress in my life. Guide me to where I can find help. Give me the courage to make the changes I need to make in order to successfully manage stress. Amen.

PRACTICE

Strive for balance in life. Make time for prayer to restore your spirit. Get enough rest. Set aside time for recreational activities that you enjoy alone or with other people. Make sure that time spent working in your profession or as a volunteer is in balance with other areas of your life.

Letting Go

There comes a point in our lives when we need to let go. Letting go of unneeded possessions helps to simplify our lives. Letting go of unrealistic expectations helps to clear our minds. Letting go of the desire to be in control helps to simplify our relationships. Letting go of unnecessary activities gives us a new sense of freedom. Letting go of the fear that bad things might happen in the future increases our trust in God. Whenever we let go, we create a new opening for the Holy

Spirit to enter into our lives and lead us in directions that we may never have chosen on our own.

PRAY

Lord, help me to recognize anything in my life that is not needed. Give me the courage to let go. Keep me open to the movement of your Holy Spirit so that I can live my life to the fullest in ways that are pleasing to you. Amen.

PRACTICE

Ask a family member or friend to help you make a personal inventory of what you need to hold on to in your life and what you need to let go. Then begin the process of simplifying your life. Look for people who might benefit from whatever you no longer need.

Maintaining Friendships

Friendships serve as a safeguard against isolation and loneliness. Friends offer us emotional support, mental stimulation, shared memories, and fun. Friendships require time, attention, and nurturing but the effort is worthwhile. Studies show that people in the second half of life who maintain friendships are happier and healthier.

PRAY

Lord, thank you for my friends. Help me to be a good friend to each one of them. Never let differences of opinion come between us. Allow us to love each other with the same unconditional love that you shower on us. Amen.

PRACTICE

Tell your friends how much they mean to you. Thank them for playing such an important role in your life. Pray for them. Ask them to pray for you.

Learning
Something New

The adage about an old dog's inability to learn new tricks is hogwash. During the second half of life, we often have the time and the financial ability to develop new skills, acquire new knowledge, and embark on new adventures. Studies show that learning something new in the second half of life is good for our memory, our mood, and our personal growth.

PRAY

Lord, give me the courage to keep learning and growing in the second half of my life. Instill in me a love of learning. Take away any fears that I might have of trying something new. Help me to find learning opportunities that will spark a new sense of fulfillment in my life. Amen.

PRACTICE

Make a list of things you have always wanted to learn. Then formulate a plan for how you can take advantage of the continuing education, lectures, book clubs, cultural opportunities, travel, and how-to classes that are available in your community. Or check out instructional videos on the internet. Think of yourself as a lifelong learner.

Reaching Out to Others

PONDER

Jesus tells us that when we do something for people in need, we do it for him (Matthew 25:31–46). Seeing Christ in others is a strong motivator for people in the second half of life who have the time and the willingness to volunteer. Reaching out to those who are less fortunate helps us to grow in compassion and mercy. It enables us to see that we are all human beings who are loved by God unconditionally.

PRAY

Lord, instill in me the desire to help other people—especially those who are in physical, emotional, or spiritual need. Help me to find opportunities to reach out to others. Give me the courage to make a commitment to help in whatever way that I can. Allow me to see you in each person I encounter. Amen.

PRACTICE

Learn more about Catholic social justice opportunities in your parish or diocese. Find out how you can offer your time, your talent, or your financial support to a local food pantry, soup kitchen, homeless shelter, or refugee center. Invite a family member or friend to join you in outreach.

The Gift
of Laughter

PONDER

Jesus assured us that he came so that his joy will be in us, and our joy will be complete (John 15:11). One of the hallmarks of Christian joy is good humor. When we hone our ability to laugh—especially at our own foibles or at amusing things that happen around us—we give ourselves a precious gift. Laughter strengthens our immune system, increases oxygen levels, reduces stress, lowers blood pressure, and makes us feel happier and healthier.

PRAY

Lord, fill me with joy. Help me to cultivate a sense of humor. Give me the courage to laugh at myself. Allow me to look for humor in my life and to respond with hearty laughter. Amen.

PRACTICE

Make a habit of laughing out loud at least once every day—even if it is fake laughter. You can encourage yourself to laugh by reading a funny story or watching a funny video. Over time, laughter will become more integrated into your daily life and you will find yourself laughing more often and more spontaneously. Seek out people who like to laugh. Whenever possible, try to bring humor into conversations.

Sharing a Smile

PONDER

Smiling has the same emotional and physical benefits as laughter. Studies show that people who smile frequently are thought of as friendlier, kinder, more competent, and more helpful. Smiles are contagious. When we smile at someone—whether we know the person or not—it almost always results in the other person smiling back. The other person experiences the same emotional and physical benefits that we experience. A simple smile could alter the course of another person's day.

PRAY

Lord, help me to see that a smile is a gift that I can share. Teach me to be generous in offering smiles to others. Allow your love to flow through me to other people in the form of a smile. Amen.

PRACTICE

Make a conscious effort to smile more often. Smile at yourself when you pass a mirror. Smile at the people you love. Smile at strangers. Smile when you sense the presence of God in your life or in the lives of people around you.

The Power of Prayer

PONDER

Our prayer does not have to be intense or lengthy. It can be as simple as recognizing God's presence throughout the course of the day. The more we enter into prayer, the more we begin to see ourselves and the people around us differently. We begin to recognize that the whole world and everything in it is God's creation. We see ourselves and other people as children of a loving God.

PRAY

Lord, instill in me a deep desire to know you and love you. Make me a person of prayer. Help me to recognize your presence throughout the day. Allow prayer to change me in ways that will make me more pleasing to you. Amen.

PRACTICE

Each morning, before you get out of bed, transform your entire day into a prayer by offering to God all that you think, do, and say during your waking moments. Make a habit of asking God to bless everyone you encounter. Thank God for all of the good things in your life and ask for strength to deal with difficulties. Before going to sleep, reflect on the ways God touched your life during the day.

Spiritual Dryness

PONDER

When we look back on our lives, we can probably recall times of spiritual dryness when prayer seemed difficult or even impossible. If we don't feel anything during prayer, it doesn't mean that we have lost our faith or that we don't love God. It doesn't mean that God has stopped loving us. It means that we are being called to persevere in faith. Remember that our desire to pray—even when we feel nothing—is in itself a powerful prayer.

PRAY
Lord, strengthen my faith during times of spiritual dryness. Help me to remain firm in my resolve to pray. Allow me to see this time of spiritual dryness as a way to grow stronger in faith, hope, and love. Amen.

PRACTICE
Talk to a friend or spiritual advisor about any difficulties you experience in prayer. Take a prayer walk through your neighborhood. Thank God for every tree and every flower. Ask God to bless the people in each home. Offer to God the spiritual dryness you feel for the conversion of people who no longer believe in God. Thank God for all of the good things in your life.

Accepting Reality

PONDER

As we get older, there are some things we can do to alter our appearance and make ourselves look younger. But there are other realities associated with aging that we cannot stop. We may encounter physical difficulties, the death of friends, and deep disappointments. When we accept reality with grace and the faith that God is with us, life becomes better. When we refuse to accept reality, life can become bitter.

PRAY

Lord, guide me through the changes I encounter in the second half of life. Help me to accept reality and make whatever modifications are necessary to live a positive and productive life. Allow me to focus on the good things in my life and be grateful for all that you continue to do for me. Amen.

PRACTICE

Make a list of the realities in your life that you cannot change. Brainstorm some creative ways that will allow you to transform those realities into something that is life-giving. Use positive affirmations such as, "Something good will happen today" or "The Lord will take care of me," to remind yourself that life is worth living.

Regrets

PONDER

Everyone makes mistakes. In the second half of life, most of us can look back on some of the choices we made and feel deep regret. We cannot change the past. If we continue to dwell on the things we should or should not have done, we may become emotionally paralyzed. It is far better to shift our focus to what we have learned from our mistakes. We can also look for any good things that may have happened in the aftermath of our mistakes.

PRAY

Lord, I am so sorry for some of the things that happened in the past. Help me to let go of anger at myself and the guilt I feel. Give me the courage to learn from my mistakes. Amen.

PRACTICE

Present your regrets to God in the sacrament of reconciliation. Feel the healing power of absolution wash away your guilt and heal you spiritually and emotionally. Follow through on whatever penance you are given and put the past behind you.

Seeking
Forgiveness

PONDER

It takes courage and humility to admit that we were wrong and to ask another person for forgiveness. The first step is accepting responsibility for what happened without rationalizations or excuses—even if what happened was unintentional. Then approach the other person with sorrow and sincerity. Acknowledge the pain this person has suffered. If the person is willing to forgive, thank God. If the person is not ready to let this go, be gracious and accepting.

PRAY

Lord, open my eyes to the pain I have caused another person. Give me the courage to ask for forgiveness. Help me to accept the consequences of my actions. Amen.

PRACTICE

Pray for the people you have hurt. Make amends in whatever way possible for what you have done or refused to do. Resolve to change your attitudes and behaviors to keep from hurting others in the same way.

Forgiving

PONDER

Forgiveness is something we do for ourselves. When we choose to forgive someone who hurt us, we let go of anger, frustration, resentment, and thoughts of revenge that can consume our souls and make us miserable. The other person may not want or deserve our forgiveness, but that doesn't matter. Forgiveness drains the poison out of our woundedness and allows us to heal. Forgiveness leads to a deep sense of peace.

PRAY

Lord, I am so wounded. Shower your healing love down on me. Help me to forgive the person who hurt me—even if that person is not seeking my forgiveness. Make me whole again in mind, body, and spirit. Amen.

PRACTICE

Let people know when they have hurt you. Ask God to help you forgive. Say an Our Father for people you are trying to forgive. If negative thoughts return, remind yourself that you have already forgiven this person. Refuse to reopen a wound that is already healing.

Listening

There is a huge difference between hearing and listening. We may hear someone's voice, but when we listen, we zero in on the essence of what the other person is saying. The older we get, the more tempted we might be to offer advice or try to solve someone else's problem. But listening—without question or comment—is an invaluable gift that we can offer to others. How well we listen to other people demonstrates the depths of our relationships.

PRAY

Open my ears, Lord, and allow me to become a good listener. Open my eyes so that I can read body language as the other person speaks. Help me to see that listening shows other people how deeply I respect and care about them. Amen.

PRACTICE

Focus totally on what another person is saying. Don't interrupt. Don't give into the temptation to think about what you are going to say next. Be aware of your own body language. Don't try to do something else while you are listening.

Sand in the Hourglass

PONDER

In the second half of life, we become acutely aware of how much sand is left in our hourglass. Once we accept that a finite amount of time remains, we can begin to live with a new freedom that allows us to appreciate each moment fully and authentically. We can take comfort in the knowledge that we came from God and we will one day return to God.

PRAY

Lord, help me to appreciate every moment of my life. Give me the courage to face the end of my life and to prepare for it in ways that will help my family members and friends deal with my eventual passing. Help me also to prepare spiritually to return to you with a grateful heart. Amen.

PRACTICE

Set priorities for what you want to do with the rest of your life. Finish things you have left undone. Get your temporal affairs in order—your will, bank accounts, investments, and insurance policies. Prepare advance medical directives and name a health care proxy. You can also specify funeral and burial preferences. Some people write their own obituary. Whatever preparations you make, you can be sure that your loved ones will be grateful.

Leaving
a Legacy

PONDER

How will you be remembered? A recent survey of people in the second half of life showed that leaving a legacy of love and moral stature was more important than a legacy of money or material possessions. You can establish a legacy by recording your deepest beliefs, teachable moments, funny stories, and most poignant moments. You can answer questions, unlock family mysteries, and provide the framework that will help younger generations make sense of their own lives.

PRAY

Lord, help me to leave a meaningful legacy. Allow me to see the meaning and purpose in my life. Give me the insight I need to leave the kind of legacy that will make a difference in the lives of my family members and friends. Amen.

PRACTICE

Create what is called an ethical will, which outlines for your family members and friends your beliefs, moral values, family history, accomplishments, regrets, personal stories, life lessons, and hopes for the future. It can be as short as a handwritten paragraph or as long as book with photos, documents, and newspaper clippings. Or you could create a video or audio tape as part of your legacy.

The Wisdom
Years

Wisdom is more than good judgment or wise thinking. Wisdom is our ability to see the world as God sees it. Sometimes, we just get a quick glimpse, but other times, we come to understand beauty, truth, mercy, and unconditional love. Not all older people become wise. But everyone in the second part of life has the opportunity to grow in wisdom. It is a choice we make. Choose the path toward wisdom.